A GIFT OF LOVE

A Gift of Love

A VOLUME OF VERSE FOR YOUNG AND OLD
AND FOR
ALL WHO HAVE SUFFERED ADVERSITY

By PERRY TANKSLEY

FLEMING H. REVELL COMPANY
OLD TAPPAN • NEW JERSEY

ISBN 0-8007-0504-1

Lovingly Dedicated
To Suzanne
and our four sons
John, Bobby, Perry and Mark

FOREWORD

The other morning, as I was walking up Fifth Avenue in Birmingham, a man about my age stopped me and said with a smile, "This is a wonderful morning."

Inasmuch as I did not know him I wondered what he was after. To my continued surprise he asked, "Aren't you glad you can walk?"

"Yes, of course," I nodded in astonishment. As he went on his way his gladness was so great that I could feel it. It was not enough for him to be able to walk or to drink in the beauty of that day. He had to share it. It really worked, too. That day I walked with a lighter step and with gladness in my heart.

Love, like gladness, must also be shared. This book, A *Gift of Love*, I believe, came from God through the artistic and creative mind and heart of one of my good friends, Perry Tanksley. As God shared with him, so the writer was unable to keep such gladness walled up in his heart. So he, with his first edition, shared with me and with many. Now we wish to share with you in this new edition.

Before you read A *Gift of Love* may I invite you to prepare your heart to receive God's love which our Heavenly Father wishes you to have. Then as you read, and with God's love in your heart, may I urge you to share with someone today. After all, love is the one gift we each can give, no matter how poor we are. Let us never forget the world is starving for love. Perhaps man's need for love is as persistent as his craving for bread. And let us remember in this mad rush to secure things that only love can satisfy the hunger of a human heart. But love, if it is to change this hate-filled world, must be seen. Will you let God's love be seen in you?

Thankful that I have had the privilege of meditating on these pages, may I now congratulate you on holding in your hand A *Gift of Love* which I warmly commend.

In His Love,
HARRY DENMAN

Nashville, Tennessee
February, 1968

"Great trials seem to be necessary preparation for great duties."—E. Thompson

A Gift of Love

"They never sought in vain that sought the Lord aright."—Robert Burns

"God had one Son on earth without sin, but never one without suffering"—Saint Augustine

"Keep your fears to yourself but share your courage with others."—Robert Louis Stevenson

TO EASE ANOTHER'S HEARTACHE
IS TO FORGET ONE'S OWN

Nearly three years ago, while passing through a deep heart-sorrow, I heard the inaudible whisper of God say, "My son, write."

"But what shall I write?" I anxiously asked.

"Write of the 'Valley of Shadows' you are passing through and write of the 'Dark Night of the Soul' of which you've known so much," He replied.

"But is that all?" I inquired.

"No!" God answered; "write of the 'Bright and Morning Star' which shines upon your path and of the Good Shepherd who leads through the 'Valley of the Shadows.'"

"But why, dear God, must I write?" I meekly begged.

He whispered, "It is in comforting others you shall find comfort and in sharing your faith, your faith will grow."

"But how can I, Lord God, who have never written before, write?" I pled.

He cried, "My son, have faith and try."

At this, my trembling fingers gripped hard a pen and slowly I began. Soon, so very soon, a poem was born. Oh, the agony and ecstasy of bringing a poem to life! That first poem entitled, "The Visitor" (page 22) was first published in the *Memphis Commercial Appeal* and thus it went around the world. Letters came from numerous states and cities and each one told of comfort and strength that brief poem conveyed. Strangely, my own troubled heart was comforted too.

Now, three years and a thousand poems later, I send forth on wings of faith and prayer, my first volume of verse. If those facing difficult grief years and souls suffering adversity and illness derive pleasure and comfort, I shall be gratified.

May these poems, out of my life and thoughts, find a lodging place in many hearts.

March, 1967   PERRY TANKSLEY

"The life of every man is a diary in which he means to write one story and writes another; and his humblest hour is when he compares the volume as it is with what he hoped to make it."—James Barrie

Love does not insist on its own way. I COR. 13:5

OH WHAT A FOOL WAS I!

Releasing butterflies
I've torn cocoons apart
But larvae always died
I tried to give a start.
I helped a bud unfold,
But noticed by and by
My fingers left a blight
That made the bud to die.
A friend who sought my love
I gave advice instead;
Oh what a fool was I!
For now our friendship's dead.

"Our sweetest songs of gratitude will not be for the troubles we have conquered, but for those we have escaped."—Amelia Barr

BEAUTY, ART AND PLEASURE

I thought life should consist
Of mostly art and pleasure,
But Life gave sorrow's cup
And I drank without measure.
I thought life should consist
Of mostly art and beauty,
But Life gave work and sweat
And I found life was duty.
Yet duty's rich reward
And sorrow's rarest treasure,
I've learned through toil and tears,
Is beauty art and pleasure.

ILLNESS SHOWS US HOW TO FACE THE FUTURE WITH FEARLESS FAITH

Why are you troubled? And why do questionings arise in your hearts? LUKE 24:38

"Christian faith is nothing else but the soul's fearless venture into the uncertain future."

FAITH SUSPENDS A BRIDGE

Don't cross your rivers 'til you come
To where your rivers are,
For faith can make them disappear
And you will journey far.
For crossing rivers in one's mind
When rivers are not real
Requires no brilliant intellect
Nor calls for special skill.
And crossing rivers in your mind
When rivers are not there,
Makes thoughts play tricks on you, and you'll
See rivers everywhere.
Don't cross your rivers 'til you come
To where your rivers are,
But when they're real, don't fear to cross;
That's what a river's for!
And you will cross each river if
Upon some rocky ridge,
Hope sinks a shaft besides the gorge
And Faith suspends a bridge.

"All I have seen teaches me to trust the Creator for all I have not seen."—Ralph Waldo Emerson

Love one another with brotherly affection; outdo one another in showing honor. ROMANS 12:10

WHERE I FOUND GOD

With scorn I built a wall
Excluding undesirables,
And I, shut-in with God,
Re-read all of my Bibles.
I had misgivings though
And so, one day in doubt
I climbed my wall to see
The things I had shut out.
'Twas there amidst outcasts
I saw the Lord of All—
The God I thought I had
Confined behind my wall.

Thus says the Lord: behold, I set before you the way of life. JER. 21:8

WASTING BREATH

If you would like to prove
What Jesus Christ can do,
Why don't you let folk see
What He can do for you?
For there's no better way
To tell of Him we trust,
Than that our friends should see
What He has done for us.
And you are wasting breath
Repeating what He taught,
If friends can't see in you
The change His Presence wrought.

GROWING OLDER IS GOD'S WILL, THERE-FORE GOOD

Do not be conformed to this world but be transformed by the renewal of your mind, that you may prove what is the will of God, what is good and acceptable and perfect. ROMANS 12:2

"Isn't the truest gratitude that which strives to widen the horizon of human happiness which has gladdened us?"—Bishop Potter

SO CHERISH UNLIVED YEARS

There's not one time in life
When all is good or bad,
For life's a blending of
The joyful and the sad.
And every phase of life
Repays in its own way,
And brings us joy enough
To brighten every day.
So cherish unlived years—
Tomorrow's path untrod—
Assured they're fragments of
The perfect will of God.

My times are in thy hands. PSALM 31:15

"Oftentimes we look with forebodings to the time of old age, forgetful that at eventide it shall be light. To many saints of old age it is the choicest season in their lives. A balmier air fans the mariner's cheek as he nears the shore of immortality; fewer waves ruffle his sea, quiet reigns, deep, still and solemn."

WHAT WOULD YOU HAVE DONE?

Greatness sometimes goes unnoticed because heroic acts of courageous men are sometimes acted out on obscure stages of life with few to witness the drama. Such may have been the case of one of my good neighbors who's gone to heaven now. With only slight knowledge of this long-ago event I, from my reluctant friend, was able to extract the following story:

"Yes, I did run for sheriff of this county at one time. That was a long time ago. I emerged victorious from the first primary and that was the beginning of my ordeal. Disreputable men representing certain illegal businesses in this county approached me concerning specific concessions and compromises they expected of every sheriff so they could continue their operation outside the law. For such immunity they promised me a pushover election and plenty of revenue, bribe money, once elected."

"What did you say?" I asked.

"Well, what could I say? I'm a Christian. I believe in the Christian way of life," he affirmed.

"But what did you tell them that day?" I asked.

"Nothing," he answered. "I pointed them to the door."

"But what did they say?" I inquired.

"They left threatening that I did not now have a chance in a million at being elected," he responded.

"Then what?" I said.

"My defeat that fall under those circumstances has brought me more satisfaction than any other so-called achievement of my life," he concluded. "It's a pillow of comfort under my aging head."

ILLNESS INTRODUCES US TO GOD IN DEEPER WAYS THAN WE HAVE EVER KNOWN

"What a debt the world owes the sufferers! Progress in every field of endeavor may be credited directly or indirectly to that army of undecorated heroes, the patient sufferers."

I MET GOD IN DEPTH

I met God in the path
Of carefree youthful days,
And in the business rush
Of feverish prosperous ways.
I met Him in the midst
Of seeking fame and wealth,
And at an altar place
And in the bloom of health.
But I, in looking back,
Am sure I did not know
My Lord in truest sense
'Til illness brought me low.
'Twas then I learned to trust
In Christ the Lord alone,
And illness showed me God
In ways I'd never known.
I'd known in casual ways
My Lord across the years,
But I met Him in depth
Through illness and through tears.

For the sake of Christ, then, I am content with weaknesses . . . and calamities; for when I am weak, then I am strong. II COR. 12:10

But he knows the way that I take; when he has tried me, I shall come forth as gold. JOB 23:10

PRESCRIPTION FOR SELF-PITY

From life's inequities
I pitied my poor self,
But all self-pity fled
When I saw one born deaf.
I wept because I had
To wear eye-glasses thick,
But when a blind man passed
I felt ashamed and sick.
I crippled on a crutch
And grieved from night 'til dawn,
But weeping ceased when I
Saw one with both legs gone.

Live in harmony with one another; do not be haughty, but associate with the lowly. ROMANS 12:16

STRENGTH IN GRIEF

When grief and sorrow cling
And will not let me loose
I've found my Bible is
To me of priceless use.
Its truth unravels all
The mystery of my need
And I find comfort there
That soothes my grief indeed.
Strength comes to me in grief
From all the scriptures say,
A lamp unto my feet,
A light upon my way.

GROWING OLDER MAY BE A TIME OF DEEP-ENING OUR DEDICATION TO GOD

But grow in the grace and knowledge of our Lord and Saviour Jesus Christ. II PETER 3:18

"The secret of a happy old age: To make the most of life as it comes, and the least of life as it goes."

GROWING OLDER

More time to pause in prayer
And on the Spirit wait,
More time to read God's word
And in it meditate.
Less urge to rush through life
With blind unheeding strides,
Less urge to prove a point,
More care to see both sides.
More grace for praising folk
Where once I sought to scold:
These are some ways I sense
That I am growing old.

"To bear pain without letting it spoil your happiness is true valor."

And your ears shall hear a word behind you saying, "This is the way, walk in it" when you turn to the right or when you turn to the left. ISAIAH 30:21

"To walk with God one must be going in God's direction and keeping in step."

"No busy man was ever miserable."

My Soul Possesses Wings

Dear Lord, don't let me be
Content with little things;
My mind has thought great thoughts;
My soul possesses wings.
Dear Lord, I will not be
Content with little thoughts,
For I have had a glimpse
Of deeds which great men wrought.
Dear Lord, I cannot be
Content with little dreams,
For I have daring plans;
My soul possesses wings.
Dear Lord, lest I should be
Content with little deeds,
Let my exploits expand
Untried and time-worn creeds.

"Faith is not belief without proof but trust without reservations."—Elton Trueblood

Men Wanted!

Of squeamish-minded men
I want to have no part,
And men with priggish views
So niggardly at heart.
For pygmy-minded men
Embracing midget goals
Squelch cherished faith from me
Just as they blight all souls.
Of stingy-minded men
My weary heart is tiring;
God, give us braver men,
Great-hearted and inspiring.

ILLNESS IS GOD'S DIVINE CALL TO THE MINISTRY OF PRAYER

A friend loveth at all times. PROVERBS 17:17

"Tribulation will not hurt you unless it hardens you."
—E. H. Chapin

UNCONFINED

Some say I am confined to bed
But I don't think they know
That though my body is shut in
I still am on the go.
I go to visit those I love
And walk to market place;
I tread the woods until it rains
And then the rainbow trace.
Of course my body cannot go
For its been ill for days,
But who would say a room confines
A soul and mind that prays?
Although my body is shut in
Through days of darkest night,
My spirit soars on wings of prayer
And moves with speed of light.
In prayer I visit those I love;
Great is the gift of prayer;
And when my thoughts are beamed toward you
You'll sense my presence there.

"No distance of place or lapse of time can lessen the friendship of those who are thoroughly persuaded of each other's worth."

"Start where you are with what you have; make something of it; never be satisfied."—George W. Carver

ONE DAY AT A TIME

I know I cannot bear
The troubles of today
With fears of future years
And guilts of yesterday.
But God does not require
That I face present years
While burdened with past sins
And crushed with future fears.
But I can live today
And make it seem sublime
By learning how to live
Just one day at a time.

"Despise not the school of sorrow. It will give you a unique part in the universal song."—George Matheson

I CAUGHT YOUR FAITH

I saw you stand steadfast in grief
But saw no trace of unbelief.
I saw you stand unmoved by stress
But saw no trace of bitterness.
I saw you stand bravely for years
But saw no trace of senseless fears.
Though you spoke not of faith's firm law,
I caught your faith by things I saw.

"I have known more of God since I came to this bed than through all my life."—Ralph Erskine

GROWING OLDER LETS US EXEMPLIFY THE LOVE WE'VE OFTEN CONCEALED

Surely the righteous shall give thanks to thy name. The upright shall dwell in thy presence. PSALM 140:13

"If I grow old beautifully I will need God's help because I have observed that those who try it alone miserably fail. In fact, only those who seek God's help succeed. I don't think I've ever seen a happy, serene and contented older person who was not a Christian."

OF THOSE GROWN OLD, THE BEST

I would in growing old
Grow kinder to my friends,
More thoughtful of their needs
And blinder to their sins.
I would in growing old
Avoid a selfish mind,
That censures everyone
With judgment so unkind.
I would in growing old
Grow in God's grace so blest,
That some would think I am
Of those grown old, the best.

. . . Let not your hearts be troubled, neither let them be afraid. JOHN 14:27

"I would like to grow to a very ripe age only if I may grow sweet and not sour, kind and not harsh, generous and not stingy, cooperative and not difficult."

"Wisdom is the right use of knowledge."

*"The highest compliment one may receive is to be told
he has a Christ-like Spirit."—Jones*

THE SPIRIT OF CHRIST

He was a craftsman good
And everything He made
Was such that those who bought
Possessed the finest grade.
He hewed plow beams so straight
That many heard of them,
And when they viewed His work,
They gladly bought from Him.
Oh, what a treasure rare,
To own one chair He made;
What greater wealth to have
The spirit He displayed.

Anyone who does not have the spirit of Christ does
not belong to him. ROMANS 8:9

HIS CALLOUSED KNEES

I love the Nazareth youth
And trust the virgin-born;
I love Christ of the cross,
The Lord of Easter morn.
But Jesus washing feet
I've loved the best and shall,
And how could one refuse
Christ girded with a towel?
And you will love Him, too
If e'er He walks your street,
And you'll know Him by knees,
Calloused from washing feet.

ILLNESS DOES NOT MEAN GOD HAS FOR-SAKEN US OR PUNISHED US

Be strong, and let your heart take courage, all you who wait for the Lord! PSALM 31:24

"The serene, silent beauty of a holy life is the most powerful influence in the world, next to the might of the Spirit of God."—G. D. Boardman

THE VISITOR

For years each day at six a.m.
He went to church and bowed his knee
And meekly prayed, "Oh God, it's Jim."
And when he'd leave we all could see
The Presence came and walked with him.
As Jim grew old the chastening rod
Of years left him so ill and drawn
His path to church is now untrod;
But in his room each day at dawn
He hears a voice, "Oh Jim, it's God!"

"When I cannot enjoy the faith of assurance, I live by the faith of adherence."—Matthew Henry

Cast me not off, forsake me not, O God of my salvation! PSALM 27:9

"Consolation indiscreetly pressed upon us when we are suffering under affliction, only serves to increase our pain and to render our grief more poignant."—Rousseau

"God will not look you over for medals, degrees or diplomas, but for scars"

PEOPLE KNOW!

Within a little town
A congregation heard
A fine evangelist
Proclaiming God's good word.
While there, the preacher met
A godly man named Jim
And when the preacher left
He wrote a card to him.
Jim's last name was unknown
So on the card he wrote,
"To Jim who walks with God"
And Jim received that note.

"I pray thee, O God, that I may be beautiful within."
—Socrates

I SMILE AT GOD

Her source of beauty rare
He sought to know one day,
And so he trailed her to
The church where she would pray.
She left with face aglow
And he spoke with a nod,
"What is your beauty's source?"
And she replied, "It's God."
He said, "Will you explain?"
She cried, "On bended knee,
Each day I smile at God,
And He smiles back at me."

GROWING OLDER IS A CHALLENGE TO KEEP OUR CURIOSITY

I came that they may have life, and have it abundantly. JOHN 10:10

"People do not lack strength, they lack will."—*Victor Hugo*

THE BEST IS YET TO BE

I gave my very best to life
For I desired to live,
And life returned with prompt reply
The best she had to give.
I lived each day as if it were
My very starting day;
With ears attuned I sought to hear
What life desired to say.
I lived each day as if it were
My final day on earth,
And life gave unreluctantly
Her cup of joy and mirth.
Indeed I gave my best to life
And life returned to me
The best she had, and with a vow,
"The best is yet to be."

"In idleness there is perpetual despair."—*Carlyle*

Why do you cry to me? Tell the people of Israel to go forward. Exodus 14:15

"There is something better than understanding God; that is trusting Him."—*Knight*

"I hardly have enough faith to be a Christian," she said. "I have no faith to ask God for favors."

"But why?" I asked.

"Because my prayers for my soldier son were all unanswered. He died a battle casualty in the recent war, you know," she replied. "God turned down my most sincere prayer."

"But God heard your prayers, didn't he?" I asked.

She replied, "Well, why didn't He let my son come back from war?"

I said, "We've rejected God's will and chosen war. Each Sunday when we repeat the Lord's Prayer we say, 'Thy kingdom come, Thy will be done on earth.' That prayer has been prayed for nearly two thousand years but it's never been fully answered."

"What's the point?" she insisted.

"As long as that prayer goes unanswered and as long as God's kingdom stays away from earth and as long as God's will is not done below, we may expect other unanswered prayers but the fault is ours," I said.

"But my boy is dead," she cried.

"Yes, but let us not blame God," I begged. "War is not His will because it does kill people, good and bad indiscriminately."

"But God could have spared Him," she cried.

"Yes," I agreed, "but God operates his world by laws, not miracles. The inevitable consequence of hate destroyed your son just as it destroyed God's Son. That's how things are here."

"Well, as I said, my faith is shattered," she sighed.

What could I say? "Please don't blame God for war and its consequence. God is love. If your heart is broken, the heart of God is shattered too," I concluded.

ILLNESS HAS A PURPOSE AND THAT PUR-
POSE IS VERY CLEAR TO GOD

The plowers plowed upon my back; they made long their furrows. PSALMS 123:3

"Why should I start at the plow of my Lord, that makes the deep furrows on my soul? I know He is no idle husbandman; He purposes a harvest."—Samuel Rutherford

THE DIVINE PLOWMAN

Most farmers never reap
No matter how they toil,
Until they first sink deep
Their plows into the soil.
For farmers are aware
To have a fruitful yield,
They must sink plowshares deep
Into each fertile field.
So God, our plowman, plows
On us until we're sore,
And though it's painful now,
Yet we need doubt no more.
For when the harvest comes
We'll thank the Lord who reaps,
And praise Him that He plowed
Upon our hearts, so deep.

"Man is never helped in his suffering by what he thinks for himself, but only by revelation of a wisdom greater than his own, it is this which lifts him out of his distress."—Carl Jung

The prayer of a righteous man has great power in its effects. JAMES 5:16

YOU HAVE A RIGHT TO DOUBT

You have a right to doubt
The deeds on sacred page
'Til Christ in you has wrought
The miracle of the age.
I knew He calmed the storm
And marched upon the sea
When He first hushed my fears
And came to walk with me.
I doubt no more He spoke
And water blushed to wine,
Since my stained heart He changed
Into His snow-white shrine.

"If Christians praised God more, the world would doubt Him less."—Charles E. Jefferson

GREATER THAN YOU DREAM

Can God who flung each star
From flaming fingertips,
Watch one so frail as I
Lest one of my feet slips?
I know the God who arched
The skies and earthly ball
And paints each lily fair
And sees each sparrow fall.
Some say, "But God's too great
To care for earth's sad scheme."
I say, "Your God's too small.
He's greater than you dream!"

GROWING OLDER MAY PROVIDE US WITH INSIGHTS TO LIFE'S PURPOSE

Ascribe to the Lord the glory due his name. PSALM 96:8

"A Christian life is not an imitation but a reproduction of the life of Christ."—Henry Van Dyke

WHO SAVES THE BEST 'TIL LAST?

Let me grow old without
Misgivings or dread fear,
For ageing is God's will
Unfolded year by year.
Why should I doubt or dread
The goodness of God's plan,
Or question things He wills
And fashions with His hand?
Then let me look ahead
Nor dote upon the past,
Assured God's will is good
Who saves the best 'til last.

"Winter is on my head but eternal spring is in my heart; I breathe at this hour the fragrance of the lilacs the violets and the roses, just as twenty years ago. The nearer I approach the end the plainer I hear around me the immortal symphonies of the worlds which invite me."—Victor Hugo

"More than the possession of courage is the power to impart it to others."

"The vocation of every man and woman is to serve other people."—Leo Tolstoy

I'm Glad I Followed

I heard Him calling me
And I obeyed and came
To champion His cause
And stand up for His name.
I soon found paths were rough
And yet through troubled days
I followed nail-scarred steps
And learned to love His ways.
I'm glad I followed Him
Though costly was the price,
And could I take it back
I'd choose again for Christ.

Bless the Lord, O my soul; and all that is within me, bless his holy name! Psalm 103:1

What Is Evangelism?

I asked, "What is evangelism?"
A poor man kindly said,
"It's like a tramp who tells
A friend where he found bread."
I asked, "What is evangelism?"
A blind youth softly sighed,
"It's like a sightless man
Who loves to praise his guide."
I asked, "What is evangelism?"
An ill man quickly told,
"It's like one snatched from death
Telling who made him whole."

ILLNESS TEACHES US TO TRUST WHEN WE CAN'T UNDERSTAND

But he knows the way that I take; when he has tried me, I shall come forth as gold. Job 23:10

"There are no crown wearers in heaven that were not cross bearers here below."—Charles Hadden Spurgeon

WHEN WE ASK WHY

They made a cross for Christ and brought
It to the place He stood;
It was a cross which hate had wrought
For one so kind and good;
A rugged cross He had not sought
But shunned as any should.
He shrunk from it as there He hung
Suspended in the sky,
And pain He bore so shocked and stung
He asked the question, "Why?"
And all the world with silence rung
But offered no reply.
And yet today from that cross gleams
A hope for souls like me,
And from the Christ a mercy streams
To all eternity;
And so, dear Lord, with shattered dreams
I humbly come to Thee.

"If you want to be miserable think much about yourself, about what you want, what you like, what respect people ought to pay to you, and what people think of you."—Charles Kingsley

For he was a good man, full of the Holy Spirit and
of faith. Acts 11:24

JUST REHEARSING

May it be said of me
When I bow from life's stage,
"He played with all his heart
  The role he should have played."
May it be said of me
When life's last curtains fall,
"He played his part with zest
  Although his part was small."
And may I hear God say
When from the stage I bow,
"Rehearsal days are done;
  Your starring role starts now."

Bravery never goes out of fashion."—William
Thackery

ATTITUDE COUNTS

Completely unaware
That I was judging him,
I watched a cripple pass
On dwarfed and twisted limb.
With pity in my heart
I seemed to hear One say,
"As you are judging him
You're being judged today."
"What do you mean?" I asked.
He cried, "Each one, indeed
Is judged by attitudes
Expressed toward souls in need."

31

GROWING OLDER MAY BECOME A PERIOD OF GROWING SWEETER

Do all things without grumbling or questioning that you might be blameless and innocent. PHILIPPIANS 2:14, 15

"Nobody grows old by merely living a number of years. People grow old by deserting their ideals."—Douglas MacArthur

MY AMBITION

I've never prayed to be
A saint when I grow old,
But in my heart I have
An even higher goal.
In my old age I hope
I'll be as kind as Christ,
And just as patient too,
No matter what the price.
I've had some friends in whom
That miracle has been wrought;
Then why can't God make me
Christlike in deed and thought?

"The price of mastery in any field is thorough preparation."

Conduct yourselves wisely toward outsiders, making the most of the time. COLOSSIANS 4:5

"That religion cannot be right that a man is worse for having."—William Penn

EARTH MUST CHOOSE BROTHERHOOD

Hats off to modern science
And scientists wise and good,
For through their skill the world
Became a neighborhood.
Science made the far-off lands
Seem like they're at our door,
And super-sonic planes
Will shrink the world much more.
Science made a neighborhood;
One choice confronts us still:
Earth must choose brotherhood
Or be a battlefield.

"Honor is a harder master than law."—M. Twain

BY THIS YOU'RE BOUND

You are not bound to win each game
But you are bound to be
The kind of soul who leaves the field
Head high and conscience-free.
You are not bound to earn each game
The victor's golden crown,
But in defeat you must stand tall;
By this you're always bound.
And you're not bound to win if it
Means win at any cost,
But you are bound to keep the rules
Though every game is lost.
Nor are you bound to win at all
If in the victory earned,
Your self-respect and honor leave
To nevermore return.

ILLNESS HELPS US TO APPRECIATE THE BLESSINGS WE ENJOY

It is good for me that I was afflicted, that I might learn thy statutes. PSALM 119:71

"It is not what happens to you but the way you take it that counts."—Hilys Jasper

UNCRIPPLED MIND

A little boy at Christmas time
Had legs all braced with steel,
But learned to use his crutches well
And one might say with skill.
He joined the crowd on Christmas morn
Who trod the path to church,
And he attached a holly wreath
Onto each sturdy crutch.
He tied some tiny Christmas bells
Onto each metal brace
And cried, "God bless us all" as smiles
Were wreathed upon his face.
"How can you smile?" one asked. He said,
"The braces that I wear
 Are on my legs, but not my mind,
 For I'm not crippled there."
"And though my legs are lame," he said,
"For life I have a plan;
 I'll give my best and hope to get
 All out of life I can!"

"They conquer who believe they can. He has not learned the lesson of life who does not each day surmount a fear."—Ralph W. Emerson

Save me, O God! For the waters have come up to my neck. I sink in deep mire where there is no foothold. PSALM 69:1, 2

THINGS WILL TURN OUT ALL RIGHT

Prior to his scheduled surgery I said to him, "Now don't you worry. Everything is going to turn out all right."

"Turn out all right?" he asked. "Then you know something my doctor doesn't know?"

"Well, not exactly," I replied. "I'm not familiar with the medical reports but I have a thorough assurance that everything is going to turn out well."

"Does that mean I'll be well soon?" he halfway asked.

"Perhaps," I answered. "Yet one cannot be perfectly sure."

"Now that's double-talk," he charged. "You're not sure whether I'll get well but still you're talking like things are going to turn out all right."

"You know." I reasoned, "our Bible says, 'In all things God works together for good to those who love the Lord.' Don't you love the Lord?"

He beamed, "You know I love the Lord!"

"Then," I continued, "this promise is for you. 'In all things'—that means in hospital experiences and exploratory operations. 'In all things God works together for good.' "

"Even if the doctor sews me back up and has to bring a negative report?" he begged.

"Sir," I said, " 'In all things'—good report or bad report, 'God works together for good.' As a Christian you are in God's will. In all things God works together for good to those who love the Lord."

"How may I also believe this and know it for sure?" he inquired.

"It's God's promise to you," I replied. "Claim this promise as your own."

GROWING OLDER MAY BE A TIME OF IN-
CREASING IN SPIRITUAL WORTH

And the peace of God, which passes all understanding,
will keep your hearts and your minds in Christ Jesus.
Philippians 4:7

"Contrary to our youth-worshipping age, the sacred
scriptures give greatest honor to old age and older
people. Surely the fashions of the age will be forgotten
but the glory and splendor of old age will ever remain."

The Golden Years

I know why latter years
Are called the golden years;
Gold is a precious gift
Wherever it appears.
Gold is a treasure rare
Which none would dare deny
Growing in elegance
As years go swiftly by.
So latter years of life
Are golden years that shine
With worth that makes me proud
Of everyone of mine.

The years of our life are threescore and ten, or even
by reason of strength, fourscore. Psalm 90:10

"The evening of a well spent life brings its lamps with
it."—Joseph Joubert

"It is the uplifted face that feels the shining of the
sun."

"The measure of a man is not the number of his servants but the number of people whom he serves."—
Moody

SELLING BREAD FOR CHRIST

"What do you do for Christ?"
  A kindly lady said.
"With my bread truck," I cried
"I fill the stores with bread!"
"Oh, that's your work!" she smiled,
"But that is not the thing.
  I mean, 'What do you do
  Each day for Christ your King?' "
I asked, "But can't I sell
  My bread in such a way
  That it becomes His work—
  A sacrament each day?"

There is great gain in godliness with contentment.
I TIMOTHY 6:6

GIVE AND YOU SHALL RECEIVE

With vision dim I led
A man all blind to light,
And my dim eyes returned
To nearly perfect sight.
With shoulders stooped and tired
I shared my neighbor's load,
And strength came back to me
As I trudged up his road.
With failing faith I prayed
For one whose faith was gone,
And faith returned to me
As silent as the dawn.

ILLNESS MAY BE A STEPPING STONE TO HIGHER BLESSEDNESS AND USEFULNESS

Guard your steps when you go to the house of God; to draw near to listen is better than to offer the sacrifice of fools. ECCL. 5:1

"With the soul that ever felt the sting of sorrow, sorrow is a sacred thing."—William Cowper

NOT "WHY" BUT "HOW"

I've left the land of "Why"
And now affirm this vow,
I go to dwell by faith
Within the land of "How."
Too long I've cried, "Why, God,
Did you do this to me?"
Henceforth I'll pray, "How, God,
May I use this for Thee?"
What happens doesn't count
And "Why" is not the test;
It's "How" I take each thing
That makes me cursed or blest.

Be not rash with your mouth, nor let your heart be hasty to utter a word before God, for God is in heaven, and you upon the earth; therefore let your words be few. ECCL. 5:2

"God brings no man into the conflicts of life to desert him. Every man has a friend in heaven whose resources are unlimited; and on Him he may call at any hour and find sympathy and assistance."—Morris

"Our main business is not to see what lies dimly at a distance but to do what lies clearly at hand."—Carlyle

You Wait And See

I said to Christ, "I quit!
What's in this work for me?"
And He just sent me back
And said, "You wait and see."
Reluctantly I turned
To my most irksome task,
But not to doubt His word
Or any question ask.
Since then I've found the task
I vainly tried to quit
Was work God planned for me,
And I've rejoiced in it.

"Many people owe the grandeur of their lives to their tremendous difficulties."—Charles Spurgeon

Great Plans

One said, "It yet remains
To see what God can do
With one who fully yields
To Christ, the Savior true."
I said, "I'll yield my life
And all I am to Thee—
And all I've ever been
And all I hope to be."
Christ said, "Then I'll bless you
Although your gifts are few;
And you'd be proud to know
Of plans I have for you."

GROWING OLDER MAY BE A TIME OF GROWING IN OPTIMISM

May we shout for joy over your victory, and in the name of our God set up our banners. PSALM 20:5

"I want to be thoroughly used up when I die, for the harder I work the more I live. I rejoice in life for its own sake."—Bernard Shaw at 90

HE'LL MAKE TOMORROW GOOD

Why should I be afraid
Of what the future holds?
For through the years I've found
God's will each day unfolds.
Just as I've faced this day
With faith that conquers fears,
So I will face with faith
The future untried years.
And I will, fearless, stride
Into those days assured
That God of yesteryear
Will make tomorrow good.

The Lord is just in all his ways, and kind in all his doings. PSALM 145:17

"I have attained my seventy-fifth birthday. You must not wonder at me even at seventy-five, eager to remain here in the high place of the missionary field, for opportunities of service were never greater and the outlook for a great harvest never brighter than now."
—Missionary Hudson Taylor writing from China.

Never flag in zeal, be aglow with the spirit, serve the Lord. ROMANS 12:11

POSTSCRIPT OF LOVE

Each dawn and noon God speaks,
And had we ears to hear it
He would reveal His love
In language of the Spirit.
And then at sunset time
At the closing of the day,
God signs His signature
In love's own golden way.
But what of darkest nights
Bejeweled with stars above?
I have deciphered them
As God's postscript of love.

He has made everything beautiful in its time; also he has put eternity into man's mind. ECCL. 3:11

THE PERFECT DAY

I felt the touch of God at dawn
And faith revived when guilt was gone.
I felt the breath of God at noon
And worries fled as love came soon.
I felt the hush of God this eve
And God's sweet peace bade tiredness leave.
Today I've dared to walk with God
And romance crowned the path I trod.

"Solitude nerves the heart for conflict."

ILLNESS TEACHES US PATIENCE, COMPASSION, AND TRUST

But I trust in thee, O Lord, I say, "Thou art my God."
PSALM 31:14

"Christianity is a battle, not a dream."—Wendell *Phillips*

MY HEART HAS BLED

Whatever friends may say of me,
Whate'er my foes have said,
They haven't told enough until
They say my heart has bled.
It seems my heart has bled enough
To make the rivers flow;
Yet from each drop that stains my path
White lilies seem to grow.
And shattered dreams that came to me,
Which bruised and crushed my heart,
Have seemed like messengers from God
With wisdom to impart.
I think it's when hearts bleed, Christ calls,
"Come share my easy yoke;"
And it is then we let Him heal
The heart that sorrow broke.
It's then we cry, "The Kingdom's Thine
Who heals our hearts that ache;
It's doubly Thine, for Your brave heart
Once on a cross did break."

We rejoice in our sufferings, knowing that suffering
produces endurance and endurance produces character
and character produces hope. ROMANS 5:4

"Jesus Christ is no security against storms, but He is perfect security in storms."

What Is Worry For?

If worry were worthwhile
Or paid a single debt,
I'm sure it would be right
To worry, fume, and fret.
If it could make it rain
Or make a person rich,
Then I would lie awake
Each night to toss and pitch.
Then what is worry for
If worry doesn't pay?
I think it's just a sign
We've failed to trust and pray.

There is no fear in love but perfect love casts out fear.
I John 4:18

Fear Slew The Rest

"I'll slay ten souls today,"
Death whispered with a grin,
"And when my sickle reaps,
I'll pass this way again!"
He came again and I
Asked Death to please explain
Why in that town he'd left
One hundred people slain.
"My plague destroyed ten lives,"
The reaper grim expressed,
"Ten times that many died,
But fear slew all the rest."

GROWING OLDER MAY BE A TIME TO SHAKE OFF PESSIMISM AND DOUBT

So we do not lose heart. Though our outward nature is wasting away, our inner nature is being renewed every day. II Cor. 4:16

"You don't grow old when you cease to grow, you are old! You don't cease to play because you grow old. You grow old because you cease to play. Your thinking does not fail because you are aging. You age only as you stop thinking."

YOUNG AT HEART

If you should say I'm old
Then I would say you're wrong;
And though my sight is dim
My heart is young and strong.
If you should think I'm old,
Don't breathe it with your tongue,
For though my back is bent
My heart is brave and young.
If you should think I'm old,
I may agree in part;
My body did grow old
But I stayed young at heart.

I consider the days of old, I remember the years long ago. PSALM 77:5

"I have often thought what a melancholy world this would be without children, and what an inhuman world without the aged."—Samuel T. Coleridge

LIFE IS WORTH LIVING

"I hardly know how to approach the subject," she began.

I waited, "Do you not wish to tell me more?"

"Actually I'm ashamed to admit it but I've been contemplating getting out of the picture," she blurted. "In other words, taking the easy way out."

Unsurprised, I calmly replied, "Desire to escape life is quite common to most everyone. Most anybody at some time or other is a candidate for self-destruction."

Sighs of relief relaxed her. "Certainly not everyone has such thoughts of exiting from life?" she asked.

"But I said 'most everyone,'" I replied. "Yes, if circumstance became unbearable enough, each of us would experience self-destructive tendencies."

"But why must I have this problem?" she inquired.

"Fear," I responded. "Moods of depression such as you are experiencing accompany deep dark fears— fear of impaired health, fear of loneliness, fear of incompetence or impotence, fear of the future and dozens of other fears."

"Yes," she nodded agreement. "But what can I do?"

"You've done a lot already," I said. "You brought it into the open. Just talking helps, you know."

"Indeed," she smiled. "Especially to know that many others are fighting this temptation, too."

"You've hit the other point," I answered.

"You must fight the temptation. At least Christ in you will help you fight these moments of frustration. Christ loves you, is with you, and is constantly reenforcing your will to live."

"I vaguely sense that," she smiled.

I concluded, "But the battle to live is likewise a battle which all must daily fight."

ILLNESS MAY REMIND US OF THOSE WHO HAVE HELPED US

So then, as we have opportunity, let us do good to all men, and especially to those who are of the household of faith. GALATIANS 6:10

"Our opportunities to do good are our talents."—Cotton Mather

I MET A MAN

When I was looking down
And bitter was my cup,
I met a man of faith
Who left me looking up.
When I was down and out
And everything went wrong,
I met a man of joy
Who left me with a song.
When I was "all done in"
And fear had drained strength out,
I met a man of faith
Who cancelled every doubt.
And I left him that day
With head uplifted high,
Thanking God for men
Who challenge and inspire.

For the Lord knows the way of the righteous but the way of the wicked will perish. PSALM 1:6

"To have known one good man—one man who through the chances and mischances of a long life, has carried his heart in his hand, like a palm tree, waving all discords into peace—helps our faith in God, in ourselves, and in each other, more than many sermons."
—George William Curtis

"Faith is a principle by which to live, not a problem to be solved."

NEW CALVARIES

In sacred Galilee
And holy Palestine
Christ made the blind to see
And water blushed to wine.
He raised the dead to life
And lame men found release,
And even on a cross
He gave an outcast peace.
Today, new crosses call
And we new calvaries climb,
That we might bless our world
As Christ blessed Palestine.

"If a man would have half his wishes, he would double his troubles."—B. Franklin

WHERE'ER HIS SHADOW FALLS

Where'er His shadow fell
Became a sacred place,
And bread He touched and blessed
Possessed a sweeter taste.
He made the deaf to hear,
The lame leaped with surprise,
Lepers He touched were cleansed
And He healed sightless eyes.
Today all bread is sweet
Blessed by the Meek and Lowly;
Where'er His shadow falls
In all of earth, seems holy.

GROWING OLDER IS A TIME TO GROW MORE INTERESTED IN LIFE

And your old men shall dream dreams. ACTS 2:17

"It is magnificent to grow old if one keeps young."—
H. E. Fosdick

NINETY YEARS YOUNG

I'm sure I'd rather be
Ninety years young, indeed,
Than forty five years old
With pessimistic creed.
For age is measured not
By time which years impart
But it is measured by
Dreams cherished in the heart.
And though I'm ninety now,
At heart I'm just a youth,
For I still dream great dreams
Of conquest, love and truth.

Six days you shall work. EXODUS 34:21

"Missionary Hudson Taylor at seventy opened a new mission field. George Mueller at ninety expanded the Bristol orphanage to care for 1500 orphans. The artist Titian painted the masterpiece, "The Battle of Lepant," when he was ninety-eight. The writer Goethe finished the classic "Faust" at eighty-two. The astronomer, Galileo, at seventy-three made some of his grandest discoveries. What about you?"

A DREAM

With whip in hand a fiend
Beat Christ 'til He slumped down,
And then he kicked Him 'til
He lay clumped on the ground.
He stomped Him 'til I wept
And when He made Him die
He turned toward me and oh!
I saw the fiend was I.

COMPENSATION

She loved the orphans' home
And often visited there,
And then one day she gave
To them her diamonds rare.
Friends say her gems are gone
But she always replies,
"I see them every day
Sparkling in children's eyes."

WHAT GOD HATH JOINED

Some live together though
They're never joined in heart,
While others bound by love
Are forced to live apart.
Some whisper marriage vows
But are not wed in mind;
Some voice no vows and yet
They're bound by love's sweet sign.

"The reward of a thing well done is to have done it."

ILLNESS MAY BE USED TO MAKE US CHRIST-LIKE IN CHARACTER

He will sit as a refiner and purifier of silver and he will purify the sons of Levi and refine them like gold and silver, till they present right offerings to the Lord. MALACHI 3:3

"The brightest crowns that are worn in heaven have been tried and smelted and polished and glorified through the furnace of affliction."—E. H. Chapin

CHOSEN FOR THE FURNACE

Affliction's rod upon my back
Has taught faith's lesson best,
And Christ who ever seeks my good
Requires I take His test.
He placed me in the furnace of
Affliction, pain, and woe,
But He's been with me all the way
Through troubled days and slow.
Soon I'll emerge like gold refined
Exposed to purging flame,
With life reflecting Jesus' love
And lips that breathe His name.

Behold, I have refined you but not like silver; I have tried you in the furnace of affliction. Is. 48:10

"Faith marches at the head of the army of progress. It is found beside the most refined life, the freest government, the profoundest philosophy, the noblest poetry, the purest humanity."—Munger

It Can't Be Done

I most admire him who can cry,
"It can't be done but I will try."
Who shouts as he his goals pursues,
"What can't be done is what I'll do!"
Who sings this song once he's begun,
"I do the things which can't be done!"
And then exclaims with joy unhid,
"What can't be done is what I did."

Take Up Your Cross

I said, "You ask too much!
A fellow has to live;
Still You come begging me
To give and give and give."
"And do I ask too much?
And does one have to live?
I had to die," He wept,
"And pray, 'Forgive, forgive.' "

The Silent Folk

The deeper streams in silence flow,
While shallow brooks still babble;
Full ships sink low and empty cars
On railroad tracks still rattle.
The silent folk like silent stars
On darkest nights shine best,
And burdened hearts like ships bowed down
Are still the ones that bless.

"Be content with what you have, never with what you are."

GROWING OLDER OFTEN INTRODUCES US TO GOD'S KEEPING POWER

The Lord be with your spirit. II TIMOTHY 4:22

"Each phase of life has certain satisfying compensations that make us know at that time that life is all worthwhile."

THE AUTUMN YEARS

No other years of life
Are ever quite so tender,
As restful autumn years
Arrayed in harvest splendor.
For feverish summer years
Have fled with work and weeping,
And though there's work to do,
Yet it is mostly reaping.
Kaleidoscopic hues
Resplendent with God's glory,
Make autumn years seem like
The best part of life's story.

And my God will supply every need of yours . . . PHIL. 4:19

"The day is done, for the fervor of shining is over, and the sun hangs golden in the West, making everything look unspeakably beautiful, with the rich effulgence which it sheds on every side. So God seems to let some people, when their duty in the world is done, hang in the West, that men may look on them and see how beautiful they are."

"Men and nations are bettered and improved by trial and refined out of broken hopes and blighted expectations."—F. W. Robertson.

SAY IT NOW

If I were sure I had
One final day on earth,
I'd spend it telling friends
How much to me they're worth.
If I were sure I had
Just one more hour grim,
I'd spend it telling friends
How much I cherish them.
I'd speak to friends of love
If I had just one minute,
But since we never know,
I'll even now begin it.

Keep your heart with all vigilance. . . . PROVERBS 4:23

ANOTHER CHANCE

Give me tomorrow, Lord,
And I'll use it for Thee,
And make You proud You gave
Tomorrow unto me.
Give me tomorrow, Lord,
For I have failed today
To do what I should do
And say what I should say.
Give me tomorrow, Lord,
And I'll return to You
A day crammed full of deeds
Which I have failed to do.

ILLNESS TEACHES US PATIENCE AND TRUST

The Lord has done great things for us; we are glad. PSALM 126:3

"Love is lovliest when embalmed in tears."—Sir Walter Scott

GETTING THROUGH THE VALLEY

When brighter days shine on my heart
As they will surely do,
And when dark clouds of woe shall rift
To let God's face shine through,
I'll not forget the lessons learned
When I could hardly see;
'Twas then I learned by faith to cling
To Him who walked with me.
When better days have dawned and I'm
No longer tempest torn,
And sorrow's night recedes as joy
Comes trailing down the morn,
I'll then recall that sorrow taught
Sweet truths I had not known,
And tears became my telescope
Through which I viewed God's throne.

Fear not, for I am with you, be not dismayed: for I am your God; I will strengthen you, I will help you, I will uphold you with my victorious right hand. ISAIAH 41:10

"Whatsoever your past has been you have a spotless future."

Rejoice in your hope, be patient in tribulation . . . ROM. 12:12

THIS IS NO HEALTH INSURANCE POLICY

Shattered health and depleted strength had left him lying on his bed as if he were glued in place.

From eyes in sunken sockets he looked up at me and pleadingly asked, "Why did this happen to me?"

Hesitantly I replied, "Trouble is no respecter of persons, it seems. Nobody is exempt, are they?"

"But I'm a life-long Christian," he snappily said.

I inquired, "But are life-long Christians released from ills and woes?"

"Well," he said, "I certainly thought being a good Christian helped a little. Doesn't that mean anything at all?"

"Yes," I replied, "but it doesn't mean what you obviously think. If Christians were exempt, all would be Christians to gain exemption from adversity. The truth of the matter is that Christians are exposed to more problems than anyone else."

"But where's all the security Jesus talked about?" he inquired.

I answered, "Jesus invited people to take up the cross. He said, 'In the world you shall have tribulations.' Often he pronounced a blessing upon His followers who would be persecuted and who would suffer for His sake. He and His early followers certainly found plenty of trouble. Being a Christian is not a health insurance policy then, is it?"

He sighed from his bed, "I'd still like to know why this all happened to me. Why? Why?"

"I don't know," I answered, "but Christ's security is not exemption from trouble. Though you may lose your health, you need not lose your faith. Amidst physical adversity Christians may experience spiritual serenity. You are secure in God's love and care."

GROWING OLDER MAY BE A TIME OF PONDERING GOD'S WILL AND GOD'S WORD

With long life I will satisfy him and show him my salvation. PSALM 91:16

"To keep young every day read a poem, hear a choice piece of music, view a fine painting and if possible, do a good action."—GOETHE

DON'T SAY I'M OLD

I say to all who think
I'm old and past my prime,
"It's just that I've been young
For a very long time."
And how have I stayed young?
Old age, to me it seems,
Can never lodge in hearts
Crammed full of faith and dreams.
I will admit I'm old
When dreams go out of style;
'Til then, say I've been young
For a long, long while.

May the Lord give strength to his people! May the Lord bless his people with peace! PSALM 29:11

"He who would pass his declining years with honor and comfort, should when young, consider that he may one day become old, and remember when he's old that he has once been young."—Joseph Addison

"Faith is the tendril by which a soul may cling to God."

"Shall I grudge to spend my life for Him who did not grudge to shed His blood for me?"—Beveridge

WHY

He could have answered words
They falsely charged Him with,
But He stood silent there,
This Man from Nazareth
He could have fled His cross
But He refused to flee
And chose instead to die,
This Man from Galilee
With spear-gashed side He hung
In utter shame and loss
That He might win a world—
Oh Man of Calvary's Cross!

"Men must have righteous principles and then they will not fail to perform virtuous actions."—Luther

I MAY BE GUILTY

With thorns they crowned my Lord
But I'm perplexed by this:
Where did those thorns spring up
Which they crowned Jesus with?
Who plucked the thorns that day?
Who made the crown and how?
Who set them on His head?
Who crushed them on His brow?
Since thorns grow in my yard
I'm made to feel at times,
'Twas I who plucked the thorns
And helped them do their crimes.

ILLNESS IS A TIME WHEN GOD EN-COURAGES US TO KEEP STRIVING

For you have need of endurance, so that you may do the will of God and receive what is promised. HEBREWS 10:36

"Sorrows are visitors that come without invitation and complaining minds send a wagon to bring their trouble home in."—Charles Spurgeon

BETTER FARTHER ON

Ready to quit, I cried,
"Oh Lord, I'm all alone"
But from the gloom He spoke,
"It's better farther on."
Bowed low in shame I wept,
"Then give me one more day!"
And instantly gloom fled
And hope dawned on my way.
And walking in that light
Nor dreading the unknown,
I've found His words were true,
"It's better farther on."

For God did not give us a spirit of timidity but a spirit of power and love and self control. II TIMOTHY 1:7

"Believe me, every man has his secret sorrows, which the world knows not; and often times we call a man cold who is only sad."—H. W. Longfellow

"God brings men into deep waters not to drown them but to cleanse them."—Aughy

"Repentance is a certain sickness of sin that makes us hate and quit it."

PETER'S REMORSE

Some think Peter's remorse
For cowardice he showed,
Caused him through life to kneel
And weep when roosters crowed.
And yet this seems opposed
To truth the scriptures teach;
When roosters crowed at dawn,
I think he rose to preach.

"The worst disappointment you can experience is disappointment in yourself."

PILATE

He hung his hand-wrought sign
Above the Saviour's head,
"Jesus, King of the Jews!"
And that is all it said.
They begged him change the sign
So it would plainly say,
"He said He was the King,"
But he refused that day.
I cannot see why he
Changed not the sign for them,
For just the night before
He'd washed his hands of Him.

"The great thing is to suffer without being discouraged."—Fenelon

GROWING OLDER MAY BE A TIME OF GROWING CLOSER TO OUR LOVED ONES

Be steadfast, immovable, always abounding in the work of the Lord, knowing that in the Lord your labor is not in vain. I Cor. 15:58

"If you have someone to love or something to do or even something to hope for, then you must not doubt God's purpose in your existence. Get busy, show love and dream dreams as long as you have breath."

You're Worth A Lot

Why say in latter years
You do not count for much?
You're worth a lot as long
As you one life can touch.
For meeting one small need
In just one person's life,
Makes you worthwhile to God
And to that friend in strife.
You're worth a lot, dear friend;
God knows the true amount.
As long as one loves you
Your latter years do count.

... I have learned in whatever state I am, to be content. Phil. 4:11

"There is not one life which the Life-giver ever loses out of His sight; not one which sins so that He casts away; not one which is not so near to Him that whatever touches it touches Him with sorrow or with joy.
—Phillips Brooks

"You cannot do a kindness too soon because you never know how soon it will be to late."

INDELIBLE RECORD

Each dawn God gives to me
A ledger all unstained,
And then he bids me write
A record clear and plain.
But whether good or bad,
I am aware each day,
My deeds recorded there
Will never pass away.
At eve I often pause
Reviewing what I wrote,
And sometimes weep because
I cannot change one note.

"A laugh is worth a hundred groans in any market."
—Charles Lamb

IN RETROSPECT

The irony of my life
Is that my earthly days
Have all been spent going
Unknown, unchosen ways,
And doing work which I
Had never planned to do,
And living in some towns
Of which I never knew.
Yet, strangely, life thus lived
Need not be life misspent,
For mine in retrospect
Seems like the life God meant.

ILLNESS MAY BE GOD'S PLAN TO BRING THE BEST OUT OF US

And I am sure that he who began a good work in you will bring it to completion at the day of Jesus Christ. PHILIPPIANS 1:6

"God from a beautiful necessity is love."—Tupper

THE SCULPTOR

"What is your task?" I plainly asked,
  And he gazed long at me
  And said with upturned head and eyes,
"Setting an angel free!"
"But I can't see an angel, Sir,"
  I answered as I stood,
  And he just chipped away and smiled,
"Oh don't you wish you could?"
  Imprisoned in our stony hearts
  An angel form resides,
  And Jesus ever seeks to carve
  His image on our lives.
  And when we cannot see a thing
  Our Master sees the good,
  And says to all who cannot see,
"Oh don't you wish you could?"

For God is at work in you, both to will and to work for his good pleasure. PHILIPPIANS 2:13

"A statue lies hidden in a block of marble and the art of statuary only clears away the superfluous matter and removes the rubbish. The figure is in the stone; the sculptor only finds it."—Addison

DOING LESS BUT BEING MORE

He timidly inquired, "Why must I feel so useless?"

I replied, "But doesn't everyone during retirement years have that useless feeling?"

"Perhaps," he answered, "but why? and how may I overcome this frustrated feeling?"

I said, "You've been the breadwinner for years; you've punched the clock, performed essential duties, earned a salary and . . ."

He interrupted, "Tell me something I don't know."

I continued, "You've been a doer, a go-getter, a worker. Your feeling of usefulness has been measured largely in terms of doing things. That phase of life for you may have passed by. Now, God gives you a new chance, not of doing something but of being something for Him."

"What do you mean, being something?" he inquired.

"Well," I answered, "God is looking for people to show patience during retirement, kindness during disappointment, contentment during discouragement, and gratitude during defeat. That is being something for God, a living example."

"But I don't see how that helps me in my discouraging circumstances of idleness and ageing," he argued.

"Well, if you'll accept your retirement years as a perfect phase of God's plan and if instead of attempting great deeds you can be content to be the salt of the earth, the light of the world, and the imitation of your Master in all things, you'll find your greatest usefulness is yet before you," I assured him.

He answered, "I'm still not sure I understand but I'm going to accept these years as God's plan, be contented, and hope God can use me."

GROWING OLDER MAY BECOME THE ONE TASK WHICH DRIVES US TO RICHER FAITH

I press on toward the goal for the prize of the upward call of God in Christ Jesus. PHILIPPIANS 3:14

"The world has forgotten that in its preoccupation with "Right" and "Left" there is an "Above" and "Below.""

NEW CHALLENGES

Life has been good to me
With all its "ups" and "downs,"
For in each phase of life
New challenges I've found.
And so my future years
Will bring me good, no doubt,
And challenge me like years
When I first started out.
So I'll rejoice in them
Nor fear the coming test,
And I will meet those years
In faith that they are best.
I've loved each challenge that
My Father ever gave,
And crave those years to prove
The glory of old age.

"They never fail who die in a great cause."—Lord Byron

"It is only through labor and prayerful effort, by grim energy and resolute courage, that we move on to better things."—Theodore Roosevelt